Penguins

by Daniel Petersburg

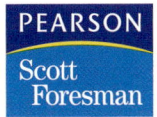

Editorial Offices: Glenview, Illinois • Parsippany, New Jersey • New York, New York
Sales Offices: Needham, Massachusetts • Duluth, Georgia • Glenview, Illinois
Coppell, Texas • Sacramento, California • Mesa, Arizona

A penguin

Penguins are birds. They lay eggs. They have wings and feathers. They have beaks. They have claws. But penguins are not like most birds.

Penguins use their wings as flippers to swim!

Penguins cannot fly. They swim! Their wings are flippers. These flippers push them forward through the water. Their feathers make penguins *waterproof*. When penguins stand on land or ice, water just rolls right off their feathers!

These penguins live in a warm place.

These penguins live in a cold, snowy place.

All penguins live in the southern half of the Earth. Most penguins live in cold, snowy places. Some live in warm places. Penguins live near the ocean. They hunt for fish. Penguins swim fast to catch the fish.

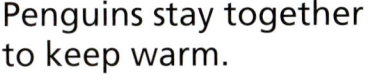

Penguins stay together to keep warm.

A penguin chick is warm under its mother.

Penguins that live in cold places need to stay warm. Penguins have a thick layer of fat under their skin. This fat helps penguins stay warm.

Penguins also work together to stay warm. They stand close to each other to stay warm.

Penguins in cold places make nests out of stones, snow, and ice. The mother lays one or two eggs. The eggs take one or two months to hatch. The chicks have soft feathers called *down*.

Penguin parents protect their chicks.

Penguins take care of their chicks. They feed them. They keep them warm. They keep them safe. Some chicks stay with their parents for two months. Some stay with their parents for a year. Then they can leave their parents. They can find food, and they can swim.

Penguins jumping into the water

A penguin sliding across the snow

Penguins have short legs so they *waddle* when they walk, moving their body from side to side. They lie on their bellies and slide on snow and ice. They jump in and out of the water. They use their flippers to help them move and swim.

Have you ever seen a penguin? Where?